2/06

Pelham Public Library
24 Village Green
Pelham, NH 03076

W9-AUI-932

FOOD CHAINS

WETLAND FOOD CHAINS

Bobbie Kalman & Kylie Burns

🌱 Crabtree Publishing Company

www.crabtreebooks.com

Created by Bobbie Kalman

Dedicated by Kylie Burns
For Dave and our three little tadpoles, Nicole, Emma, and Alex, who keep us hopping!

Editor-in-Chief
Bobbie Kalman

Writing team
Bobbie Kalman
Kylie Burns

Substantive editor
Kathryn Smithyman

Project editor
Molly Aloian

Editors
Michael Hodge
Robin Johnson
Kelley MacAulay

Design
Katherine Kantor
Margaret Amy Salter (cover)

Production coordinator
Heather Fitzpatrick

Photo research
Crystal Foxton

Consultant
Patricia Loesche, Ph.D., Animal Behavior Program, Department of Psychology, University of Washington

Illustrations
Barbara Bedell: pages 3 (mink and earthworm), 9 (mink), 11 (mink), 15, 25 (middle), 27 (raccoon, crayfish, and grasshopper)
Katherine Kantor: pages 3 (snake, mosquitos, cattails, and heron), 9 (fish), 11 (deer and cattails), 25 (top), 27 (snake), 29
Bonna Rouse: pages 3 (beaver, swan, avocet, and lily pad), 10, 11 (goose and lily pad), 13, 27 (frog)
Margaret Amy Salter: pages 9 (plant), 11 (plants), 25 (bottom), 27 (plants)
Tiffany Wybouw: page 3 (frog)

Photographs
© Jerry Segraves. Image from BigStockPhoto.com: page 21
Bruce Coleman Inc.: Jean-Claude Carton: page 20
© CDC: James Gathany: page 23
iStockphoto.com: pages 4 (bottom), 6 (bottom), 8, 14
© Dwight Kuhn: page 24
Photo Researchers, Inc.: E. R. Degginger: page 15; Jerome Wexler: page 12
robertmccaw.com: pages 5, 16, 17, 22 (bottom), 30
Visuals Unlimited: Steve Maslowski: page 26
Other images by Corel, Digital Stock, and Digital Vision

Library and Archives Canada Cataloguing in Publication
Kalman, Bobbie, date.
    Wetland food chains / Bobbie Kalman & Kylie Burns.

(Food chains)
ISBN-13: 978-0-7787-1953-3 (bound)
ISBN-10: 0-7787-1953-7 (bound)
ISBN-13: 978-0-7787-1999-1 (pbk.)
ISBN-10: 0-7787-1999-5 (pbk.)
    1. Marsh ecology--Juvenile literature. 2. Food chains (Ecology)--
Juvenile literature. I. Burns, Kylie II. Title. III. Series: Food chains

QH541.5.M3K34 2006   j577.68'16   C2006-904076-1

Library of Congress Cataloging-in-Publication Data
Kalman, Bobbie.
    Wetland food chains / Bobbie Kalman & Kylie Burns.
        p. cm. -- (Food chains)
ISBN-13: 978-0-7787-1953-3 (rlb)
ISBN-10: 0-7787-1953-7 (rlb)
ISBN-13: 978-0-7787-1999-1 (pb)
ISBN-10: 0-7787-1999-5 (pb)
    1. Marsh ecology--Juvenile literature. 2. Food chains (Ecology)--
Juvenile literature. I. Burns, Kylie. II. Title. III. Series.
QH541.5.M3K348 2007
577.68'16--dc22

2006021839

Crabtree Publishing Company

www.crabtreebooks.com   1-800-387-7650

Copyright © **2007 CRABTREE PUBLISHING COMPANY.** All rights reserved. No part of this publication may be reproduced, stored in a retrieval system or be transmitted in any form or by any means, electronic, mechanical, photocopying, recording, or otherwise, without the prior written permission of Crabtree Publishing Company. In Canada: We acknowledge the financial support of the Government of Canada through the Book Publishing Industry Development Program (BPIDP) for our publishing activities.

Published in Canada
Crabtree Publishing
616 Welland Ave.
St. Catharines, ON
L2M 5V6

Published in the United States
Crabtree Publishing
PMB16A
350 Fifth Ave., Suite 3308
New York, NY 10118

Published in the United Kingdom
Crabtree Publishing
White Cross Mills
High Town, Lancaster
LA1 4XS

Published in Australia
Crabtree Publishing
386 Mt. Alexander Rd.
Ascot Vale (Melbourne)
VIC 3032

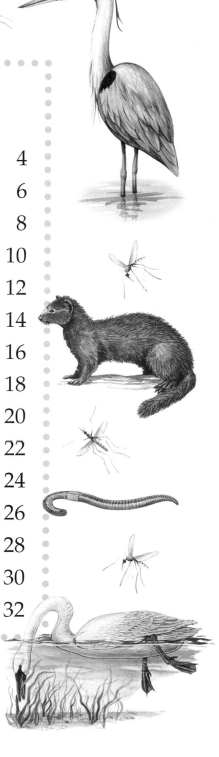

Contents

What are wetlands?

*A **swamp** is a wetland that has trees and shrubs growing in it.*

*A **fen** is a wetland that is not always covered with water.*

Wetlands are areas of land that are covered with water. Some wetlands are covered with water year round. Others are covered with water only at certain times of the year. The soil in wetlands is **waterlogged**. Waterlogged soil is soaked with water.

Salty or fresh

Wetlands can be found in most places on Earth. They often form where lakes, rivers, or oceans meet land. Near lakes and rivers, wetlands contain **fresh water**. Fresh water has only a little salt in it. Near oceans, wetlands have **salt water**. Salt water has a lot of salt in it.

Freshwater marshes

A **marsh** is a kind of wetland. Marshes are covered with water all year long. Some marshes contain salt water, whereas others contain fresh water. This book is about freshwater marshes.

Aquatic plants

Many **species**, or types, of **aquatic plants** grow in marshes. Aquatic plants are plants that grow in or near water. Sawgrasses, cattails, and water lilies are some aquatic plants.

Trees do not grow in marshes, but they often grow near the edges of marshes.

Marsh animals

Marshes are habitats for amphibians such as frogs.

This dragonfly is a marsh insect. It searches for other insects to eat in marshes.

Marshes are **habitats** for many species of animals. A habitat is a natural place where plants and animals live. Fish, birds, **reptiles**, and **amphibians** live in marshes. Amphibians are animals that live part of their lives in water and part of their lives on land. Many kinds of insects live in marshes, too!

At home in a marsh

Different animals live in different parts of a marsh. Some animals, such as fish, live in the water. Other marsh animals, including many species of birds, live on land, but they eat the plants and animals that live in water.

Residents and visitors

Some animals do not spend their entire lives in marshes. They visit marshes to find water and food. Many species of birds **migrate**. To migrate is to travel long distances to new habitats when the seasons change. Some birds, including the Canada geese shown right, visit several marshes as they migrate. They stop at marshes to rest, drink, and eat as they travel between their summer and winter habitats.

Part-time residents

In parts of the world that have hot summers and cold winters, many species of birds live in marshes for only part of the year. Red-winged blackbirds are part-time residents in marshes. During spring and summer, a red-winged blackbird lives in a marsh. When the weather turns cold in autumn, the bird migrates to another habitat. The red-winged blackbird then returns to the same marsh in spring.

What is a food chain?

Plants and animals are living things that need air, sunlight, water, and food to survive. Living things get **nutrients** from food. Nutrients are substances that keep living things healthy. Living things also get **energy** from food. Plants need energy to grow. Animals need energy to move, to breathe, to grow, and to find food.

Plants produce food

Green plants **produce**, or make, food using air, sunlight, and water. They change energy from the sun into nutrients. Plants use some of the energy and store the rest.

These marsh marigolds are using air, sunlight, and water to make food and to grow.

Animals eat food

Animals cannot produce food. They must eat to get nutrients and energy. Some animals eat plants. Animals that eat only plants are called **herbivores**. Other animals, called **carnivores**, get nutrients and energy by eating animals.

An energy chain

The energy that green plants produce passes to the herbivores that eat the plants. When the herbivores are eaten by carnivores, some of the energy passes to the carnivores. This pattern of eating and being eaten is called a **food chain**. Every plant and animal belongs to at least one food chain.

Starting with the sun

Green plants use the sun's energy to make food. They use some of the energy and store the rest.

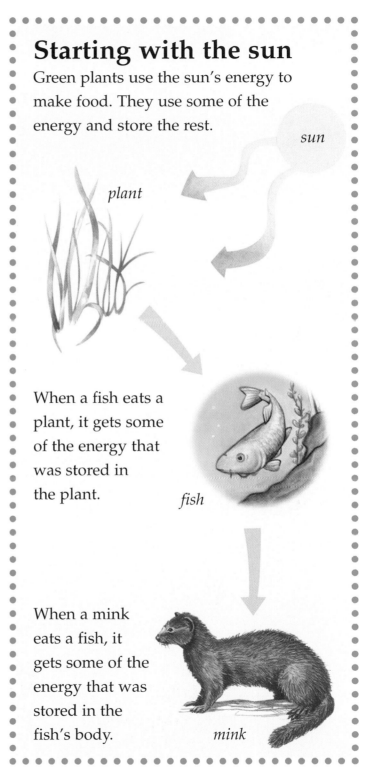

sun

plant

When a fish eats a plant, it gets some of the energy that was stored in the plant.

fish

When a mink eats a fish, it gets some of the energy that was stored in the fish's body.

mink

Levels in a food chain

A food chain is made up of three levels. The three levels are plants, herbivores, and carnivores.

First level

The first level is made up of plants. Plants are living things that have stems, roots, and leaves. They are called **primary producers**. Plants are the **primary**, or first, level in a food chain because they produce their own food. Primary producers called **algae** are also part of marsh food chains. Algae live in water. They are not plants because they do not have stems, roots, and leaves. Algae use the sun's energy to make food just as plants do. As a result, algae are often called "plants."

Second level

The second level in a food chain is made up of herbivores. Herbivores are called **primary consumers** because they are the first living things in a food chain to **consume**, or eat, food instead of making it from the sun.

Third level

The third level of a food chain is made up of carnivores. Carnivores are known as **secondary consumers** because they are the second animals to consume food in a food chain.

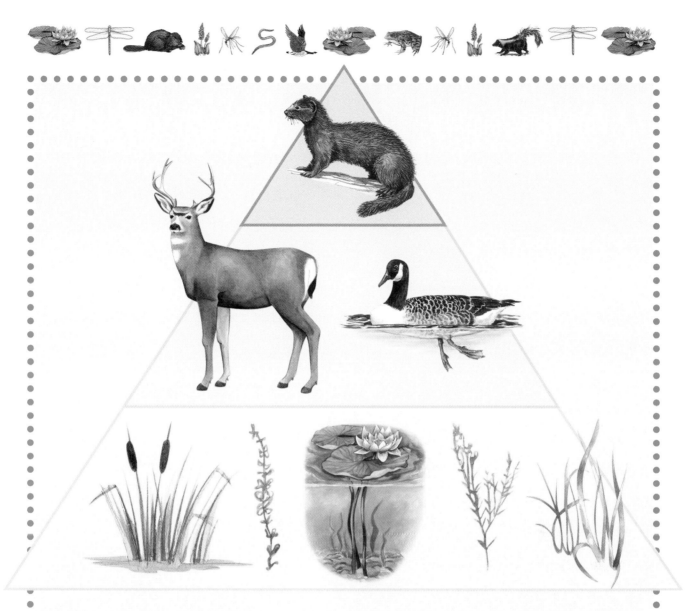

The energy pyramid

This **energy pyramid** shows the movement of energy in a food chain. A pyramid is wide at the bottom and narrow at the top. The first level of an energy pyramid is wide to show that there are a lot of plants. The second level of the pyramid is narrower because there are fewer herbivores than there are plants. Herbivores get only some of the sun's energy when they eat plants. The third level shows that there are fewer carnivores than there are herbivores. Carnivores get less of the sun's energy than herbivores do.

Food from sunlight

Plants and algae can make food because they contain **chlorophyll**. Chlorophyll is a green **pigment**, or color, that takes in the sun's energy. In plants and algae, chlorophyll combines the sun's energy with water and **carbon dioxide** to make food. Carbon dioxide is a gas in air and water. The food that plants and algae make is a sugary substance called **glucose**. The process of plants turning air, sunlight, and water into food is called **photosynthesis**.

There is green algae growing on the water in this marsh. The algae is making glucose.

Sunlit water

Sunlight can travel through marsh water. Marsh water is also shallow enough for sunlight to reach the aquatic plants that grow on the bottom of marshes. Aquatic plants and algae **absorb**, or take in, sunlight during photosynthesis.

Making oxygen

During photosynthesis, aquatic plants and algae also absorb carbon dioxide from water and air. As plants and algae make food, they turn carbon dioxide into **oxygen**. Oxygen is a gas that animals need to breathe. Plants and algae release the oxygen into the water and air.

A plant's leaves absorb carbon dioxide from water and air.

Chlorophyll absorbs the sun's energy.

As a plant makes food, it releases oxygen into water and air.

13

Plants and algae

Only certain species of plants can grow in waterlogged soil. Dry soil contains pockets of air, which plants need to survive. Plants that live in dry soil absorb some air through their roots. In marshes, the soil is so full of water that there is little room for air. Aquatic plants have parts that help them get enough air. For example, some aquatic plants, such as cattails, are **emergents**. Emergents are plants with roots that grow in waterlogged soil. Emergents also have parts that stick up out of the water. The stems of emergents are **hollow**. These hollow stems carry air down to the underwater parts of the plants.

Some aquatic plants have parts that float on the surface of the water to take in air. The leaves of water lilies float on the surface.

14

Underwater plants

Aquatic plants called **submergents** grow under water. Submergents do not need air. They have thin, feathery leaves that absorb carbon dioxide from water. Coontail, shown right, and pondweed are two types of submergents that grow in marshes.

Phytoplankton

Phytoplankton are the smallest algae. They are so tiny that they can be seen only through a microscope! Phytoplankton float near the surface of the water. There are billions of phytoplankton floating in a marsh. Many marsh animals eat phytoplankton.

Marsh herbivores

Many herbivores live in marshes. **Zooplankton** are the smallest herbivores. They are tiny animals that float in water. Zooplankton eat phytoplankton. Other marsh herbivores include tadpoles, snails, and certain species of fish and insects. These animals eat algae and underwater plants. Moose, deer, geese, and beavers are also herbivores that live in marshes. Like most herbivores, they eat many types of plants. Moose and deer eat emergents such as cattails and grasses. Geese dive under water to eat submergents such as **water milfoil**. Beavers feed on the bark and roots of trees that grow around marshes.

*Beavers also eat **cambium**. Cambium is the soft tissue under the bark of trees.*

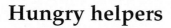

Hungry helpers

Herbivores, such as this moose, help protect marshes by eating plants. Marsh plants grow and spread quickly. Without herbivores, marsh plants would grow so close together that they would take up all the space in marshes. They would also absorb all the water. Soon, the marshes would become dry and many animal species would die.

Grinding teeth

The shape of an animal's teeth shows what it eats. Herbivores such as deer and mice have mostly flat teeth for grinding plants. Many herbivores grind food by moving their teeth from side to side. Beavers have flat back teeth for grinding, but they also have long, sharp front teeth for cutting through bark.

17

Marsh carnivores

Carnivores help control the **populations** of herbivores in marshes. Without carnivores, the populations of many kinds of herbivores would grow too large. The herbivores would eat all the marsh plants! Many marsh birds are carnivores.

Egrets, kingfishers, owls, and hawks are carnivores that hunt and eat fish, insects, frogs, and small mammals. Other marsh carnivores include frogs, snakes, and raccoons.

The kingfisher shown above is a carnivore. It has caught a small fish to eat.

18

The third consumers

Carnivores that hunt and eat herbivores are secondary consumers. Birds, turtles, and certain species of fish are secondary consumers. Some marsh animals are called **tertiary consumers**.

The word "tertiary" means "third." Tertiary consumers are carnivores that eat other carnivores, so they are the third consumers in a food chain. Some birds, minks, large fish, and snapping turtles are tertiary consumers.

Two in one

Certain marsh carnivores can be both secondary and tertiary consumers. An egret, such as the one shown above, is a secondary consumer when it eats a mouse, which is a marsh herbivore. The egret is a tertiary consumer when it eats a carnivore, such as a snake or a frog, which eats herbivores.

A frog has a sticky tongue. It uses its tongue to catch insects. The frog's sticky tongue shoots out quickly and catches insects as they fly nearby. Using its sticky tongue, this frog has caught a large dragonfly.

Most marsh carnivores are **predators**. A predator is an animal that hunts and eats other animals. The animals that predators hunt are called **prey**.

Made to hunt

Many predators have bodies that are made for hunting. For example, snapping turtles hunt by waiting in the muddy soil at the bottom of marshes for prey to swim past. They have eyes on the top of their heads so they can see prey swimming overhead. When prey swim near snapping turtles, the snapping turtles **ambush** them! To ambush means to attack by surprise.

Camouflage

Some marsh animals have **camouflage**. Animals with camouflage have colors, textures, or patterns on their bodies that help the animals blend in with their surroundings. Camouflaged predators are able to sneak up on prey without being noticed. It is difficult for predators to see camouflaged prey, however. Bitterns have feathers with stripes and spots that blend in with reeds. When bitterns sense danger, they stretch their necks and move slightly from side to side. When they move this way, they blend in with the swaying reeds and are difficult to see.

Bitterns hide among reeds and wait for prey such as insects, small birds, and mice.

21

Marsh omnivores

Some marsh animals are **omnivores**. Omnivores eat both plants and animals. Crayfish, foxes, skunks, and some insects are marsh omnivores.

This skunk has caught a snake to eat.

Rarely hungry

Omnivores are often called **opportunistic feeders**. Opportunistic feeders are animals that eat any food they find. Omnivores hunt when prey are nearby, but they also eat seeds, fruit, and leaves. In winter, marsh animals often have trouble finding enough food to eat. Omnivores, such as the snapping turtle shown left, are less likely to go hungry than are carnivores or herbivores!

Food for mosquitoes

Male mosquitoes are herbivores. They drink only fruit juices and **nectar**. Female mosquitoes drink nectar, too. The females of some mosquito species drink fruit juices, nectar, and the blood of other animals. These female mosquitoes are omnivores. Animal blood contains nutrients that the females need to lay their eggs.

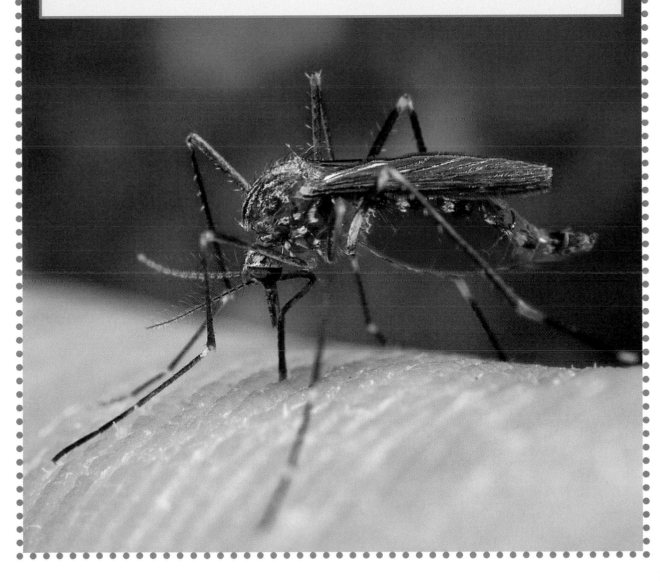

Eating marsh leftovers

Some marsh animals are **scavengers**. Scavengers are animals that eat **carrion**, or dead animals. Vultures are scavengers. These birds fly high in the sky looking for carrion. When they spot a predator eating an animal, they wait until the predator has finished eating and then swoop down to eat whatever meat is left.

They eat anything!

Crayfish are omnivores. They are also scavengers. Crayfish eat rotting plants. They also eat the leftover meat on dead animals. By eating dead plants and leftover meat, scavengers use the nutrients in the plants and animals that would otherwise go to waste. By eating carrion, scavengers help keep marshes clean.

Crayfish eat shrimp, fish, worms, insects, snails, and water plants. They also eat dead animals—even other crayfish!

24

Decomposers

Scavengers are not the only animals that use leftover nutrients. Animals called **decomposers** keep soil healthy by eating **detritus**, or dead plants and animals. By eating detritus, decomposers release nutrients back into the soil through their waste. Plants cannot grow unless the soil contains nutrients. Without plants, there would be no food for herbivores. If there were no herbivores, carnivores would starve.

Nature's recyclers

Bacteria are tiny decomposers that can be seen only with a microscope. Earthworms and snails are other marsh decomposers. Decomposers are part of **detritus food chains**.

A detritus food chain

When a plant or an animal, such as this muskrat, dies, its body becomes dead material in soil.

Decomposers in the soil, such as this earthworm, eat the dead material. They use some of the nutrients. They release the rest of the nutrients in their waste into the soil.

The nutrients in the soil help plants grow.

Note: The arrows point toward the living things that receive nutrients.

A marsh food web

Most species of marsh animals eat a variety of foods. As a result, these animals belong to more than one food chain. When an animal from one food chain eats a plant or an animal from another food chain, two food chains connect. Connected food chains form a **food web**. A food web shows how the animals that live in a habitat are connected to one another. There are many food webs in a marsh.

Fish belong to many food chains. They eat algae, plants, insects, and other fish. Their predators include birds, turtles, frogs, and muskrats.

Energy in the web

This diagram shows how living things form a marsh food web. The arrows point toward the living things that are receiving energy.

Raccoons eat northern water snakes, frogs, and crayfish.

Northern water snakes eat frogs and crayfish.

Crayfish eat plants and grasshoppers.

Grasshoppers eat plants.

Frogs eat grasshoppers and other insects.

plants

Marshes in trouble

Fertilizers and other harmful substances have polluted the water in which these fish once lived.

Stop growing!

Fertilizers are chemicals that help plants grow. People use fertilizers on their lawns, gardens, and crops. When it rains, fertilizers mix with water and flow into marshes. Once in a marsh, fertilizers cause many plants to grow. In fact, often so many plants grow that they take up all the space and use up all the water. Soon, the marsh becomes dry.

Marshes around the world are being threatened by the actions of people. People **drain** the water from marshes to create dry land. They use the land for farms, roads, and homes. When marshes are drained, some marsh animals move to other habitats. Most of the plants and animals die, however.

Pollution

When people **pollute** marshes with detergents, oil, and **fertilizers**, they poison marsh plants and animals. These harmful substances flow from marsh water into many other waterways and poison those habitats, too.

Introduced species

People sometimes take plants or animals from one habitat and place them in another habitat. Plants and animals that are moved into new habitats are called **introduced species**.

On the loose

Some introduced species are not part of marsh food chains. For example, purple loosestrife, shown right, is an introduced species of plant found in marshes across North America. North American marsh animals do not eat purple loosestrife. As a result, it grows quickly and crowds out many plants that marsh herbivores eat. Without plants they can eat, marsh herbivores cannot survive.

Introduced carp

Carp are fish that were introduced to North American marshes over one hundred years ago. Few marsh carnivores eat carp, so the number of carp in marshes grew quickly. Carp eat underwater plants. They have eaten so many marsh plants that some plant species no longer exist.

29

Protecting marshes

Marshes and other wetlands are habitats for many species of plants and animals. They also provide places for migrating animals to rest and to find food. More and more people are working to protect marshes. Some people belong to **conservation groups** that provide people with important information about marshes and how to help protect them. Many marshes and other wetlands are **conservation lands**. Conservation lands are areas of land that governments protect from harm. Laws protect both the lands and the plants and animals living on the lands. Draining marshes and other wetlands in protected areas is **illegal**, or against the law.

How to help

There are websites, videos, and other books that provide all kinds of information about marshes and other wetlands. Use these resources to find out what you and your family can do to reduce water pollution and keep marshes and other wetlands healthy.

Encourage your parents and other adults to stop using fertilizers on their lawns or gardens. Learn about programs in your area that help protect wetlands. Some groups organize wetland cleanup projects. The people in the picture below are cleaning up a wetland.

Glossary

Note: Boldfaced words that are defined in the text may not appear in the glossary.

conservation groups Groups of people who join together to protect living things from harm

drain To cause water to run out of a place

emergent A water plant with leaves and flowers that appear above the water in which the plant grows

energy The power living things get from food, which helps them move, grow, and stay healthy

fertilizers Chemicals that people put into soil to help plants grow

hollow Describing something with a hole or empty space inside

nectar A sweet liquid found in flowers

pollute To make an area dirty by adding garbage or other substances that are harmful or poisonous to the environment

population The total number of one species of plant or animal living in a certain area

reptile A cold-blooded animal with dry, scaly skin—snakes, turtles, and lizards are reptiles

water milfoil A water plant with feathery underwater leaves

Index

Printed in the U.S.A.